*A
Planning Guide
For High School Students*

· by Helen H. Heron

EAST CHICAGO PUBLIC LIBRARY
EAST CHICAGO, INDIANA

HERON PUBLISHING • LIVERMORE, CALIFORNIA

Library of Congress Number: 91-090666
ISBN 1-880639-24-6

Published by Heron Publishing
977 East Stanley Boulevard, Suite 230
Livermore, California 94550

Copyright ©1989, by Helen H. Heron.

All rights reserved. No part of this publication may be
reproduced, stored in a retrieval system, or transmitted,
in any form or by any means, including electronic,
mechanical, or photographical, without the prior written
permission of the author, except for the inclusion
of brief quotations in a review.

First Printing, December 1989
Second Printing, July 1991, Revised
Third Printing, April 1992, Revised

Distributed by Momentum Associates, Ltd.
Post Office Box 12266
Glendale, California 91224-0966

Edited by Lisa H. Smith
Designed by Angelo Mou

To Zelda, Rosemary, and Janie, who helped make this possible.

CONTENTS

Introduction **8**
Leaving Elementary School **10**
Elementary School Summary Pages **11**
Planning Your High School Experience **16**
Activities And Sports **18**
High School Summary Pages **21**
Vocational Training **37**
College Goals And Tests **39**

- **43** Resume Work Sheet
- **49** College Selection
- **55** College Application And Scholarships
- **59** Developing Listening Skills
- **61** Picking A Major And Setting Goals
- **65** Goal Setting Work Sheet

July Checklist **69**
School Choice Work Sheet **71**
August Checklist **75**
Managing Time **77**
Time Work Sheet **79**
September Checklist **83**

Test-Taking Tips **85**
Letters Of Recommendation **87**
October Checklist **89**
Developing Essays **91**
Essay Work Sheet **93**
November Checklist **97**
Learning Styles **99**
Memorizing With Ease **101**

- **105** December Checklist
- **107** Financial Aid Hints
- **109** Financial Aid Work Sheet
- **111** January Checklist
- **113** Note-Taking Tips
- **115** February Checklist
- **117** Reducing Stress

March Checklist **119**
Research Skills **121**
April Checklist **123**
Problem Solving **125**
May Checklist **127**
Reading Skills **129**
June Checklist **131**
Summary **134**
Bibliography **136**

"*Books are the quietest and most constant of friends: they are the most accessible and wisest of counselors, and the most patient of teachers.*"

Charles W. Eliot, *The Happy Life*

INTRODUCTION

College Countdown will help you successfully plan for college and complete the application process. It is divided into two general areas. The first part gives you an overview of the whole planning process:

- Picking A College
- Picking A Major
- Setting Goals
- Financial Aid
- Scholarships

Specific questions and study guides for each month will help you learn essential skills:

- Managing Time
- Taking Tests
- Developing Essays
- Memorizing
- Taking Notes
- Reducing Stress
- Doing Research
- Problem Solving
- Reading Effectively

Work sheets will reliably help you make choices appropriate for you. Finally, checklists will give you the deadlines you must meet each month, the year before you enter college.

Enjoy this creative problem-solving approach, designed to make the college application process easier!

LEAVING ELEMENTARY SCHOOL

As you leave elementary school, it is time to think about those things you enjoy doing, and also about your hopes and dreams. You need to record your accomplishments during elementary school to remind you about the things you did well and enjoyed.

During the summer between 8th and 9th grades, try to complete a typing course. Learning to type will mean that you are a step ahead in keyboard skills to computer word process your high school papers. You will find that most schools and public libraries have computers for your use.

Summarizing your elementary school activities is a good step to assist you in planning your high school classes and activities. Use the following work sheet to record your elementary school experience. This work sheet summary will help you see what you have accomplished.

When you enter high school, you should receive a high school class guide and list of student activities. Referring to the work sheet will aid you in selecting high school classes and activities which focus on what you enjoy and emphasize what you hope to add to your list of accomplishments in high school as preparation for college and the career of choice.

Show your elementary school summary to your parents and discuss your feelings about high school with them. They will help you set your high school goals.

ELEMENTARY SCHOOL SUMMARY

EIGHTH GRADE

Teacher:

School:

Address:

Classes Taken:	Grades:

School Activities:

Leadership Positions:

Sports:

Clubs:

Awards:

Summer Schools:

School Publications:

Arts, Crafts, Photography, Music:

Auto Shop, Wood Shop:

Graduation Honors:

Outside School Activities:

Sports and Hobbies:

Trips:

Club and Church Activities:

My high school goals:

PLANNING HIGH SCHOOL

What Classes Should I Take?

Before you enter high school, you should review a list of classes and activities that you have enjoyed in elementary school and compare it with a list of your high school's required courses and elective choices.

You should plan to take all of the courses required for college admission, even if you are undecided now about attending college. You may change your mind! Typical colleges and universities require:

- Fine Arts — 1 year
- Foreign Language — 2 years
- Science and Lab — 2 years
- Mathematics — 3 years
- Social Studies — 3 years
- English — 4 years

What Should I Keep In Mind?

If you have a specific college or university you want to attend, you should ask the Director of Admissions for a list of high school courses required for admission into that institution.

Remember that state colleges may have a different combination of required high school courses, while many community colleges may require only a high school graduation certificate or require that the applicant be at least 18 years of age.

To make your high school experience a delightful one, check with your high school counselors every year and take notes on their advice. As you discover new interests and abilities, you may want to change to electives that will help you explore future career and hobby choices. You may also wish to explore the wonderful opportunity of taking college and university classes for credit during your high school summers. These classes can help you learn even more in areas which interest you, as well as introducing you to a college environment.

As you plan your high school and summer activities, remember that you are not expected to do everything. You have the freedom to pick and choose activities that you enjoy and do more of them!

MY COUNSELOR'S ADVICE

ACTIVITIES AND SPORTS

As you start high school, plan activities and sports that will make you look your best to the college you eventually want to attend.

As an incoming freshman, you will need to plan your high school career by participating in those activities that will help colleges know your goals and interests are focused because you have clearly defined them and have been working on accomplishing them.

Starting in the 9th grade and working through the 12th grade, some of the special classes and activities that show you have special talents and abilities include:

Writing
Join the staff of the yearbook or the school newspaper staff. Enter writing and essay contests. Compose speeches for contests and debate tournaments.

Art and Drama
Enroll in special design, drawing, painting, ceramic, and pottery classes. Act in school plays, musicals, and in community theaters.

Music
Participate in school orchestras, bands, choirs, madrigal groups, musicals, junior symphonies, summer music camps, music award competitions, and church choirs.

Photography
Work on the photo staff of the yearbook or the school newspaper. Publish in city or local newspapers. Win awards at local art shows and county fairs.

Sports
Be an active team player in the events you like best. Follow a regular training program to develop above-average skills.

Agriculture
Join future Farmers of America or 4-H Clubs. Enter state and county fairs to gain award recognition.

Home Economics
Work hard and compete for awards and prizes at county, state, and national fairs. Offer to help a local business in your area of interest.

Technical Arts
Volunteer for "helper" experience at auto and body shops, metal shops, manufacturers, and engineering or architectural firms.

Business
Participate in Future Businessmen of America, Junior Achievement, and Regional Occupation Programs.

Leadership

Become an Eagle Scout or join clubs such as Junior Statesmen or Key Club. Apply to be a legislative page. Work for your senator, congressman, assemblyman, city councilman, or for local civic and charity organizations.

I want to participate in these high school activities and sports:

HIGH SCHOOL SUMMARY

NINTH GRADE

Counselor:

School:

Address:

Classes Taken:					Grades:

School Activities:

Student Government:

Sports:

Clubs:

Awards:

Summer Schools:

School Publications:

Arts, Crafts, Photography, Music:

Business Programs:

_____

_____

Special Activities (Dances, Homecoming, Etc.):

_____

_____

Outside School Activities:

Employment and Volunteer Work:

_____

_____

Club and Church Activities:

_____

_____

Sports and Travels:

_____

_____

_____

What I want to accomplish in tenth grade:

MY COUNSELOR'S ADVICE

HIGH SCHOOL SUMMARY

TENTH GRADE

Counselor:

School:

Address:

Classes Taken: Grades:

School Activities:

Student Government:

Sports:

Clubs:

Awards:

Summer Schools:

School Publications:

Arts, Crafts, Photography, Music:

Business Programs:

_____

_____

Special Activities (Dances, Homecoming, Etc.):

_____

_____

_____

Outside School Activities:

Employment and Volunteer Work:

_____

_____

Club and Church Activities:

_____

_____

Sports and Travels:

_____

_____

What I want to accomplish in eleventh grade:

_____

_____

_____

_____

_____

_____

MY COUNSELOR'S ADVICE

HIGH SCHOOL SUMMARY

ELEVENTH GRADE

Counselor:

School:

Address:

Classes Taken: Grades:

School Activities:

Student Government:

Sports:

Clubs:

Awards:

Summer Schools:

School Publications:

Arts, Crafts, Photography, Music:

Business Programs:

_____

_____

Special Activities (Dances, Homecoming, Etc.):

_____

_____

_____

Outside School Activities:

Employment and Volunteer Work:

_____

_____

Club and Church Activities:

_____

_____

Sports and Travels:

_____

_____

_____

What I want to accomplish in twelfth grade:

MY COUNSELOR'S ADVICE

HIGH SCHOOL SUMMARY

TWELFTH GRADE

Counselor:

School:

Address:

Classes Taken: Grades:

School Activities:

Student Government:

Sports:

Clubs:

Awards:

Summer Schools:

School Publications:

Arts, Crafts, Photography, Music:

Business Programs:

Special Activities (Dances, Homecoming, Etc.):

Outside School Activities:

Employment and Volunteer Work:

Club and Church Activities:

Sports and Travels:

Your experiences in high school will be ones for you to recall as you grow older.

Keep records to jog your memory and give you perspective about your formative, school years. You will probably want to refer to them for many personal reasons. In other cases, you will want them to verify what you have accomplished. It is recommended that you safely keep the below listed records, among others:

- High school diploma.
- Grade and class transcripts.
- Award certificates and medals.
- Photographs.
- Newspaper articles.
- Yearbooks.
- College application essays.
- Letters of recommendation from your teachers.
- Summer school or extra-curricular course completion certificates.

You may even wish to keep this book as a diary of what you thought in your teenage years!

VOCATIONAL TRAINING

Some students have career goals in business, service companies, or manufacturing in mind, but do not want to go to a full, four-year college. If you are one of them, you should check with your school counseling office because you may want to start work as soon as possible after graduation, and perhaps return for further training later. Schools offer some fantastic vocational opportunities through Regional Occupation Programs, which offer everything from cooking, butchery, auto shop, and bank services to cosmetology and computer science skills.

While you are in high school, you may also participate in Work Experience Programs where you may hold a regular job, with pay, and earn high school graduation units as you work. In your junior year, you may even take work-related classes at your local community college and explore other options in your particular community.

Life-long Learning:
Adult and Vocational Education

Life-long learning includes all education, often at colleges, that does not lead to a Bachelor's Degree or college graduation. It includes everything from one-day seminars to two or three-year programs taken after high school.

Examples of life-long learning schools range from beauty colleges to truck driving, broadcasting, computer science, and management training schools.

In the '90's and leading into the 21st century, job market analysts indicate that the need for people to be trained and retrained in different areas of expertise will substantially increase, along with the number of schools offering continuing education.

Qualifications:

Adult and vocational education schools, both public and private, assume that you have a high school degree or a **GED**. Some schools will admit you if you are ready to take the **GED**, or perhaps will even prepare you for the **GED**. Most schools give a simple admission test that corresponds to the courses the applicant wishes to take. Vocational schools want you to succeed, get a good job, and be an advertisement for them.

Class Schedules:

Admission to classes may be at the start of a school term, on a quarter or semester basis, or even every week or day for individualized units. This type of system is called "open entry" and saves you from waiting to learn job skills you need to immediately enter or re-enter the job market.

Loans For Life-long Learning:

You may apply for federal scholarships if you can prove that you have the "ability to benefit" from vocational or continuing instruction. For shorter-term schooling, some schools may even grant you a loan and let you pay it back after you have a job, or, if you are already working, your employer may have a program to pay for your special training.

COLLEGE GOALS AND TESTS

As you go through high school and begin the process of choosing a college outlined in this book, start by asking yourself what your goals and purposes are. Students want to go to college for a variety of reasons:

- Develop talents and natural abilities.

- Qualify for specific professions or careers.

- Learn to make informed professional decisions.

- Meet people and make connections.

- Gain a general education.

- Acquire information and special skills.

Every year during high school, you will need to progress toward making your final college applications. Part of gaining admission into colleges and universities is taking tests which determine your abilities and interests. With the help of your teachers or counselors and the catalogs, you will be able to schedule dates for taking the standard admission tests required by most colleges and universities:

- Preliminary Scholastic Aptitude Test (PSAT)

- Scholastic Aptitude Test (SAT)

- American College Testing (ACT)

- College Achievement Tests (ACH)

- Advanced Placement Tests (AP)

Think of your sophomore year as a year to practice taking the Scholastic Aptitude Tests, American College Tests, and College Achievement Tests.

In your junior year, make sure you schedule the Preliminary Scholastic Aptitude Test, the basis for awarding National Merit Scholarships, as well as other tests necessary for your upcoming college application. Additional tests include the Advance Placement Test which may qualify you for course credits at some colleges.

By the first half of your senior year, you should have taken all of the tests required for your application to the colleges and universities of your choice. If you take some of the required tests more than once, your highest scores should be submitted.

Before your senior year, check with your counselor to confirm that you are on your way to fulfilling graduation and testing requirements and meeting the particular entrance requirements for each college or university you may wish to attend after high school. It is best to write colleges and universities and request college catalogs from the Directors of Admission to keep you in touch with current information.

To help you on your way to college, remember that you will need to keep a record of your major high school achievements. The resume that follows will help you summarize your accomplishments and determine what your purposes are in going to college.

Once you have completed the following resume, give it to the teachers in your areas of interest who gave you an "A" and who will say something positive about you personally, when they are asked to write letters of recommendation to accompany your college applications. As a reminder for your teachers, check back with them before each college's deadlines to be sure they wrote and mailed your letters on time.

Ask your teachers for good letters of recommendation and don't be embarrassed. It is part of their jobs to help you. Remember not to ask teachers just because you like them: Select teachers who will give you the strongest recommendations! A Certificate of Mailing will prove you sent your forms on time.

MY COUNSELOR'S ADVICE

Your resume will help your teachers write your letters of recommendation for both college applications and scholarships. In addition, you may use the information to write autobiographical essays required by some colleges and universities.

What Is My Academic Record?

Grade Point Average: _____   Class Rank: _____

Test Scores:

    PSAT _____   SAT _____

    ACT _____   ACH _____

Achievement Tests:

_____

_____

Advanced Placement Tests:

_____

_____

Which Awards Have I Won?

_____

_____

_____

RESUME WORK SHEET

Honors:

Fine Arts:

Vocational Classes:

My Easiest Subjects Are:

My Favorite Subjects Are:

What Activities Have I Pursued?

Student Government Offices And Committees:

School Clubs, Offices, And Committees:

Publications:

School Sports:

School Drama, Art, Music:

Outside Clubs, Offices, And Activities:

Community Volunteer Groups, Religious Activities:

Travel:

Hobbies And Interests:

Difficulties And Problems Overcome:

Employment:

My purpose in going to college is:

COLLEGE SELECTION

Your first couple of years in college will be an excellent opportunity for you to explore various fields of interest and career choices before you decide on a major. If you are undecided, choose a liberal arts college with many strong departments in which you may begin your studies with an undeclared major. If you are attracted to a particular area of study, you should apply to colleges or universities that have excellent academic reputations in your chosen discipline.

During July and August before your senior year in high school, you should visit the colleges that interest you. The following chapters and work sheets will help you set criteria for determining which college is best for you: large or small, co-ed, near or far, challenging or comfortable, and, most of all, will you fit in? If you should "fall in love" with a particular school, you will be inspired to work for excellent grades to get admitted!

What Types Of Colleges Are There?

In choosing the right college, you should know that most colleges (except community colleges) have entrance requirements which include a combination of grade point averages, test scores on Scholastic Aptitude Tests (**SAT**), Achievement Tests (**ACH**), or American College Tests (**ACT**), and letters of personal recommendation. Ask your counseling office or public library for a guide to colleges to evaluate which ones you may qualify to attend.

If you rank in a school's top 5% for admission in grade point averages and test scores, you will probably meet the qualifications for that college. If you rank in the bottom 5%, your chances of admission to that college will be poor. Study hard and plan for success, not failure! There are many college choices in America: community colleges, state colleges, state universities, and private schools. Their positive and negative aspects are listed on the following pages to help you evaluate them.

Remember that you may apply to as many schools as you like. Keep your options open:

- Apply to two schools that are "sure" admission.

- Apply to two where you rank in their "middle range."

- Apply to two "wish" schools.

COMMUNITY COLLEGES

Pro:

- Have no entrance requirements (anyone admitted at age 18).

- Provide courses you may have missed in high school.

- Offer an Associate of Arts (AA) degree in two years so you may begin to work.

- Help you complete the first two years of college before you transfer to a four-year school.

- Are the least expensive choice for education after high school.

- Offer the opportunity to live at home and commute to school.

- Have smaller class sizes and tutorial centers.

- Provide individual counseling for personal and scheduling problems.

Con:

- Have many classes that may not transfer for degree credit.

- Offer much the same environment as high school.

- Are usually less demanding academically.

- Offer a more limited choice of classes.

- Make forming long-term relationships more difficult than a four-year institution.

STATE COLLEGES

Pro:

- Often have particularly good departments in specific fields of study.

- Provide a place to fulfill general academic requirements during the first two years without declaring a major.

- Offer the opportunity to develop long-term friendships during a four-year period.

- Have excellent reputations which increase chances of acceptance to graduate school.

- Advanced degree continuation at the same location into master's degree programs.

- Are less expensive than universities and private schools.

- Frequently have tutorial and counseling centers.

Con:

- May have weak departments which could affect acceptance into some graduate schools.

- Are larger and more impersonal than community colleges.

- Require high school graduation unless exceptional circumstances are present.

- Have entrance requirements that combine grade point averages and **ACT** test scores.

STATE UNIVERSITIES

Con:

- Have the highest entrance requirements and academic standards in a state.

- Are the most expensive of higher education institutions.

- Are large and impersonal.

Pro:

- Are the most competitive schools in each state.

- Have many strong departments and broad fields of study.

- Offer a diverse cultural environment.

- Have graduate schools which grant master's degrees and Ph.D's.

- Provide dormitory or apartment life-transitions away from family.

PRIVATE SCHOOLS

Con:

- May have high tuition.

- May encourage social cliques, limiting personal growth.

- May lack a diverse student body and broad cultural environment.

- May have social or religious values that conflict with your own.

Pro:

- Typically make a commitment to the students to do everything in their power to ensure success.

- Range from no selectivity to the most competitive in academic standards for admission.

- Frequently have a lower student-to-teacher ratio.

- Most offer dormitory life focused on mastering adult social skills and developing cohesive social groups.

COLLEGE APPLICATION AND SCHOLARSHIPS

The application process takes six months from beginning to end. Begin by writing to several schools that meet your criteria. If you apply to about six, you can stay on top of the paperwork and limit your expenses for application fees, although some application fees may be waived or excused if you demonstrate financial need.

As you receive the forms, mark in the absolute deadlines and then back up the deadlines a week to make sure you will be on time. Be sure you have carefully noted deadlines for all of the forms, letters of recommendation, essays, transcripts, and for taking tests required by each college or university.

How Do You Apply For Scholarships?

Most scholarships are based on financial need as defined by the Financial Aid Form (**FAF**) or Student Aid Application in California (**SAAC**). These forms should be available in your high school counseling office and must be completed by your parents because they are based on your parents' income tax forms and also factor in the number of children, house payments, business and medical expenses, and other variables.

The **FAF** application will help you apply for a full range of scholarships and grants. There are specific scholarships for categories such as ancestry, parents occupation, major chosen, civic participation, individual college private grants, excellent academic records, and high college test scores.

Discuss the possibilities with your high school counselor to see which ones may be an opportunity for you, including National Merit Scholarships which are awarded, based upon your junior year test scores on the Preliminary Scholastic Aptitude Test (**PSAT**).

Many awards are given for scholarship potential, not financial need alone. It is important for you to apply for these scholarships and awards, even if you believe that you will not qualify because of financial need.

Many schools award the honor of the scholarship to the most academically qualified students and the actual money to lower scoring students who really need the money. However, some prizes and awards may be won by entering competitions. Here also, financial need is not the sole criteria. You should check with your high school's counseling office regularly for new scholarship offerings and the specifics for each. When you write to colleges and universities for catalogs and admission information, don't forget to also request information on any grants and scholarships offered by each institution.

Your college application and testing process will fill lots of your time the first-half of your senior year. You will need to study for special tests, schedule the time to take them, and even re-schedule them if you want another chance to improve your scores. Remember to pick your test dates carefully to avoid scheduling conflicts.

You will also need to plan time for requesting and sending information to colleges and universities, in addition to keeping up with your normal class studies and regular activities. The monthly checklists and reminders in this book will help you to organize and plan wisely. Use them constantly, along with the space provided for your personal notes!

The Final Decision

By mid-January, you will have submitted all of your required college application materials. In response, some schools may offer you an Early Decision Option and grant you early admission. Before accepting any offers, you should review your original criteria for selecting a college with your parents. Although accepting may reduce your anxiety, it may commit you to a choice that will be difficult to change later, if you should decide that another college or university is better for you. Remember that most letters of acceptance will not arrive until mid-March though mid-April of your last semester in high school.

When you receive your acceptance letters, look at the financial aid package offered. This will typically be a combination of scholarships and grants (which do not need to be repaid), work study programs, and student loan terms and conditions. You will want to choose a combination scholarship and loan package that will give you the most "free" money and the least amount of loans to be repaid. Remember that many banks also offer student loans which you may use to supplement additional financial need.

Think about enjoying your upcoming experiences. Most colleges and universities will want your letter of acceptance by May 1st!

MY PARENT'S ADVICE

DEVELOPING LISTENING SKILLS

Throughout high school and college, you will be interacting more heavily with teachers, counselors, and other people. It is important that you develop evaluative listening skills to help you determine what information is important for you to use and remember. This study guide will help you to sharpen your ability to listen well!

Interacting With People:

- Let people know you are listening by focusing your attention on what they are saying, taking notes, or looking at them.

- Respond by paraphrasing; this shows that you comprehend.

- Give and seek opinions to clarify and expand upon ideas.

Analyzing Information:

- Analyze what has been said by comparing and categorizing data and ideas.

- Summarize, elaborate, and integrate what has been said with other data and ideas to synthesize creative, new ideas.

- Develop criteria for evaluating what you are hearing and then analyze information and interpretations to accept or reject points made by the speaker.

- Listen and take notes for definitions, main ideas, and details.

- Record procedures, processes, or strategies on how to do an assignment.

Looking for Motivations:

- Define the speaker's intentions and motives.

- Judge the speaker's completeness and accuracy, whether or not you agree.

- Separate facts from opinions and inferences.

- Develop logical conclusions from your assessments.

PICKING A MAJOR AND SETTING GOALS

Picking a major that's right for you will take some investigation. You should review college and university selection guides available at your public library or school counseling office. Once you have received your college test scores, you should review them to see if your scores reveal strengths in the major you are considering.

The following Goal Setting and School Choice Work Sheets will ask you questions to help you determine your areas of interest in picking a major and a college.

Investigate how the school will prepare you for your educational goals:

- Inquire if the school is co-ed or not.
- Check to see if it has sororities and fraternities.
- Decide if you want to live near or far away from home.
- Imagine yourself participating in the sports and recreation available if there is snow, sea, or sunshine.

Visit the campuses and talk to attending students or talk to alumni:

- Confirm that you like the people and the look of the campus.

- Ask if you would fit in on each campus.

- Check to see if you think that the dormitories would be a pleasant place to live and study.

Consider whether or not a school meets your needs and desires:

- Are there strong departments in your proposed majors?

- Is the college or university accredited?

- Are special tutoring and honors programs provided?

Complete this exercise in visualizing to help you pick a major and brainstorm goals. Before you begin, find a place where you can be uninterrupted for thirty minutes and have a tablet handy to write down your experiences. Start by breathing deeply a few times and then ask yourself:

- Which classes interest me the most?

- Which are the most fun?

- Which are the easiest?

Next, imagine the person you admire most (your mentor) walking down a path with you:

- See yourself asking your mentor to list your best qualities.

- Listen while he or she reminds you of six or more personal qualities you have that your family or favorite teacher has discussed with you.

Now, ask yourself, "If there were no limits of time and money what would I most like to do using my strengths?":

- See yourself ten years from now doing those things.

- Feel how the job would be when you felt unwell.

And, finally, ask your mentor which of these professions would pay the best and continue to exist in a changing world:

- Ask your mentor to suggest courses and extra-curricular activities that would prepare you for that career.

- Plan to participate in these activities and classes.

- Are there any practical problems? Discuss with your mentor how to overcome them.

Borrow your mentor's glasses. Look through them to see yourself studying and succeeding in school and in your life!

GOAL SETTING

What do I want from my college experience?
Here are some questions you should answer
to help you clarify your reasons for wanting to go to college.
Your goals and reasons will become the criteria
you use in choosing a group of institutions for which you wish to apply.
The questions will help you select the final school you will attend.
Answer the questions in detail to make the wisest choice.
Be honest with yourself!

Why do I want a general education?

_____

_____

_____

_____

Why do I want to experience new and different situations?

_____

_____

_____

_____

What specific talents and skills do I want to develop?

_____

How will I meet people and make connections?

How do I want to prepare for a specific career or profession?

By joining civic or business organizations?

By attending church activities?

By helping friends?

By meeting challenges?

By attending summer school?

When I dream, I imagine myself accomplishing the following goals in my life:

JULY CHECKLIST

1. Apply for your Social Security Card, if you do not have one.

2.

3.

4. Begin your college visits.

5.

6. Pick your major.

7.

8.

9. Study: Developing Listening Skills.

10.

11.

12.

13.

14.

15. Continue college visits.

16	17 Review: Developing Listening Skills.	18
19	20	21 Brainstorm your college goals.
22 Complete your Goal Setting Work Sheet.	23	24 Plan more college visits in the fall.
25	26	27
28	29 Complete your School Choice Work Sheet.	30 / 31

Spending your time considering schools will expand your horizons. These questions will help you develop a description of the college or university that is best for you. Your goal should be to find the school where you can best develop morally, intellectually, emotionally, and socially. Choosing six schools for your consideration will make your final decision easier!

SCHOOL CHOICES

What size schools would I like best?

500? _____

1,000? _____

10,000? _____

50,000? _____

What are the advantages of a co-educational college or university for me?

_____

_____

_____

_____

Why do I want to live near home or commute?

_____

_____

Why do I want to live away from home, even in another state?

Will I want to live in a dormitory or in an apartment?
(Dormitories may save time, but apartments give freedom of choice and more privacy.)

Why might I want to live in a big city?
(Big cities are cultural centers for art, music, drama, and sports, but also have problems with housing, transportation, and crime.)

Why might I want to live in a smaller community?
(Smaller communities have more space, sports, and a more relaxed environment, but are often isolated and have fewer cultural offerings.)

I will choose my most "challenging" schools from among:

I will choose my most "comfortable" schools from among:

I will choose my "sure admission" schools from among:

My final list of six colleges:

AUGUST CHECKLIST

1 Discuss your college choices with your parents.	**2**	**3** Look into college classes for credit during your senior year.
4	**5**	**6**
7	**8** Study: Managing Your Time.	**9**
10	**11**	**12**
13	**14**	**15** Consider any new college choices.

16	17 Get letters of recommendation from summer employers.	18
19 Review: Managing Your Time.	20	21
22	23 Complete your Time Work Sheet.	24
25	26	27 Review your college choices.
28	29 Plan fall activities to enhance your resume.	30 / 31

MANAGING TIME

As you enter high school and work toward college, you will need to learn to manage your time more effectively. Carefully study the list below for hints on time management. Developing time management skills will assist you in becoming more productive at school and at home. You will find yourself becoming more organized.

Be honest when you fill-in your personal time schedule:

- Mark relaxation and recreation time on your calendar, including holidays, dances, sports, and family events.

- Plan your time schedule around your class schedule, including labs, practice sessions, and performances.

- Record dates for your mid-terms, finals, tests, quizzes, and note due dates for major essays, which you should begin writing up to three weeks in advance.

- Note due dates for major essays and give yourself reminders to begin well in advance.

- Use flash cards at least three to five times a day in bursts of five to ten minutes for memorizing.

- Keep your time schedule flexible, as the demands on your time may change.

Be realistic when you plan to control your study time:

- Allow time for unexpected events, sickness, and business or personal emergencies.

- Give yourself adequate time for attending to personal needs, such as meals, sleep, grooming, transportation, exercise, and household chores.

- Figure in work time if you have a job and remember to include time for getting to and from work.

- Revise your weekly schedules to accurately reflect the actual time you spend on various activities.

TIME WORK SHEET

As your senior year unfolds, you may want to have a large calendar for your room with plenty of space for you to record all college application related events and deadlines. To make a large calendar, use a two-foot by three-foot piece of poster board and line-off the appropriate months, weeks, and days, starting with September and ending with April. Take the catalogs of the six colleges or universities you chose, and, one at a time, write in the deadlines for each category listed below. Be thorough. The monthly activity calendars elsewhere in this book will help you!

Catalog Requests:

Application Forms:

Scholarship Forms:

Test Registration Dates:

Actual Test Dates:

College Applications:

Application Supporting Materials:

College Essays:

High School Transcripts:

Letters of Recommendation:

Scholarship Forms:

Financial Aid Forms:

Other Requested Information:

SEPTEMBER CHECKLIST

1 Organize your school schedule.

2

3 Check your high school graduation requirements.

4

5 Check your college entrance requirements.

6

7 Request college catalogs and admission, and scholarship forms.

8

9 Plan to enter award competitions.

10

11

12 Send Certificate of Mailing for **ACT** October test date.

13

14 Check for scholarships listed in your counseling office.

15

16 Send Certificate of Mailing for **ACH** October test date.	**17**	**18**
19 Participate in vocational interest surveys.	**20**	**21** Study: Test-Taking Tips.
22	**23** Make appointments with visiting college reps.	**24**
25 Write in deadlines for college forms as you receive them.	**26**	**27**
28	**29** Review: Test-Taking Tips.	**30**

TEST-TAKING TIPS

Before A Test:

- Check the time and place for testing.

- Sleep at least six hours the night before and eat properly.

- Set aside at least two, #2 pencils with erasers, two pens, and paper.

- Study special materials that will help you increase your scores.

- Plan to take unwrapped candy with you to keep up your blood sugar level.

At The Start Of A Test:

- Read test directions carefully and understand precisely what you are being instructed to do.

- Glance over the entire test and divide up your time wisely to allow you to complete each section.

- Make a quick outline for all essays before starting to write them.

- Use relaxation techniques to keep you focused and alert.

Multiple Choice Questions:

- Answer the questions you know rapidly and make small checks next to the ones you will skip to answer later.

- Go back and answer skipped questions by eliminating wrong answers. Reason logically.

- Measure, count, and check models carefully.

- Follow the time allotment per question to maximize your score.

- Double-check your answers and erase any margin checks or notes.

- Fill in the answer bubbles with only two or three strokes. Polishing bubbles wastes time.

- Scan your answers to make sure that they correspond to the correctly numbered bubbles.

LETTERS OF RECOMMENDATION

Choose teachers to write letters of recommendation who taught you in your area of interest and gave you an "A." Pick teachers who will say something positive about you and who taught you in your junior or senior years. Remember to give teachers a copy of your resume to remind them of all of your accomplishments!

Teachers To Ask:

Names of Schools: **Deadlines:**

Don't be embarrassed to ask teachers if they feel that they can write good letters of recommendation for you. As a courtesy, be sure to give each teacher a stamped, addressed envelope for every college on your list. Politely remind them of deadlines and check back with them a week before letters are due to make sure they'll be on time.

Other letters of recommendation may be requested from your freshman and sophomore year teachers, employers who thought you did an excellent job, respected alumni of the colleges or universities you wish to attend, and distinguished civic or church leaders.

Keep copies of all of these letters for your files.
You may need them later!

OCTOBER CHECKLIST

1 Update your resume.	**2** Juniors should schedule the **PSAT** for National Merit Scholarships and Awards.	**3** Note college form deadlines on your calendar.
4	**5** Request letters of recommendation from teachers and others.	**6**
7 Discuss college goals with your counselor.	**8**	**9** Match your high school credits with requirements for each college.
10	**11** Study for the October **SAT**.	**12**
13 Study: Developing Essays.	**14**	**15** Send Certificate of Mailing for English Achievement Tests with Composition.

16	17 Review: Developing Essays.	18
19 Begin writing your college essays.	20	21 Follow-up with teachers on deadlines for letters of recommendation.
22 Study for October **ACT**.	23	24 Show your college essays to teachers and parents for suggestions.
25 Fill out college application forms.	26	27 Finish writing and typing college application essays.
28	29 Send Certificate of Mailing for **SAT, ACT, ACH** December test dates.	30 / 31

DEVELOPING ESSAYS

During high school and college, you will be asked to write many essays on different subjects. Your college application essay will probably be an autobiographical one. Use the facts from your Resume Work Sheet and these guidelines to help you!

Achieving Good Organization:

- Focus precisely on the set topic.
- Brainstorm ideas and write a detailed outline.
- Think of creative, new ways to explain the topic.
- Write your first draft.
- Set the draft aside for several days before revising it.

Revising The First Draft:

- Read your paper out loud to yourself.
- Verify that your ideas strictly pertain to the topic.
- Analyze whether or not your outline is logical and coherent.

- Read each paragraph for accuracy of facts and examples.

- Ask your parents and an English teacher to review your essay for improvements.

Attending To Details:

- Be sure your language is simple, straightforward, and concrete.

- Check punctuation, capitalization, and spelling.

- Evaluate grammar, including word choices, subject-verb agreement, tenses, and sentence structures.

- Type the paper perfectly with adequate spacing and correct margins.

- Double-check that your name is on the paper and that any other required information is included.

ESSAY WORK SHEET

Most college and university application essays are autobiographical in nature, but specific topics do vary! When writing an autobiographical essay, you need to think carefully about who you really are and what factors have shaped you. The questions asked below will help you with your definition of yourself.

What is special about me?

What are my strengths?

What motivates me?

What are my character traits?

What kind of work habits do I have?

What experiences do I treasure?

What have I achieved to prove my strengths?

What are my professional and personal interests?

What are my career and personal goals?

What activities do I like to participate in?

What specific difficulties have I overcome?

Be sure you understand your essay topic before you begin. Using your answers to all of the above questions will help you develop a thesis statement. The purpose of your thesis statement should be to catch the attention of college admission committees. Remember to ask a teacher and your parents for suggestions. Do have them check your essay before you submit it. Most college and university essays are autobiographical, but specific topics do vary! Often, you will be able to adapt your original essay for different schools.

My thesis statement is:

Main points that back up my thesis are:

NOVEMBER CHECKLIST

1	**2** Study for November **SAT** and **ACH**.	**3**
4 Check deadlines for mid-term college entrance in January.	**5**	**6** Double-check your college essay for accuracy.
7	**8** Tell teachers to mail letters of recommendation.	**9**
10	**11** Complete final list of college application choices.	**12**
13 Double-check all college application deadlines.	**14**	**15** Request sixth semester transcripts if required by colleges.

16	**17** Complete all applications to your college choices.	**18**
19 Check community college deadlines.	**20**	**21** Send all college applications Certificate of Mailing.
22	**23** Study: Memorizing With Ease.	**24**
25 Study for December **SAT, ACT,** and **ACH** test dates.	**26**	**27**
28	**29** Review: Memorizing With Ease.	**30**

LEARNING STYLES

As you prepare for college, you will be processing more and more information. Using the learning methods that work for you will help you score your best on your high school and college tests. Decide what learning styles benefit you the most and stick with them!

The Visual Learner:

Do you have to read to remember material? Do you use flash cards to memorize? Do you doodle, draw diagrams, or pictures? Does it help you to color code your notes? Can you visualize (see in your mind) how a room looks without furniture? Can you visualize how clothes will look on you without trying them on? Answering "yes" to these questions indicates that you learn by seeing.

The Auditory Learner:

Do you have to hear a lecture or a discussion to remember your lessons? Do you have to say things out loud to memorize? Do audio tapes help you learn? Can you remember a song the first time you hear it? Does it help you if you teach someone else? Answering "yes" to most of these questions indicates that you learn through hearing.

The Tactile Learner:

Do you have to "do" a process to learn it? Do you have to write down the spelling of words to remember them? Do you write lists? Do you draw objects or ideas in the air? Do you write on your leg? Do you have to experience something to comprehend it? Answering "yes" to most of these questions indicates that you learn by touching.

Knowing how you learn best will be invaluable information for you to use during the rest of your life. Spend some time thinking honestly about the following questions. You will understand a lot more about who you are!

- What combination of seeing, hearing, writing, and experiencing is best for me?

- What happens when I memorize by making associations or connections?

- How does it help me when I visualize a process or event?

- Does it help me to memorize when I make up rhymes?

- Do I take ten minute breaks every hour when I am studying?

- Does playing calm, background music while I am studying help my memory?

- Does my studying seem to improve when I exercise vigorously before hand?

- Does eating real food, not junk food, before I study keep me more alert?

MEMORIZING WITH EASE

Scheduling Brief Sessions:

- Memorize three times a day for 10 to 15 minutes.

- Focus on 2 to 7 bits of new information at one time.

- Use flash cards or concise lists to help you.

Memory Methods:

- Make up a joke, rhyme, or an acronym (a word made up of the first letters of each word in your "phrases to memorize" list).

- Connect each fact with a room in your house or parts of a car.

- Associate facts with counting 1, 2, 3, 4, 5, 6, 7, etc.

- See it, say it, write it.

Visual Aids:

- Imagine scenes happen in history, as if you were there or as in the movies.

- Associate key words with your five senses.

- Trace a flow chart for processes or anatomy.

- Draw mathematics and science formulae in different colors.

Auditory Aids:

- Recall your teacher's voice explaining main points.

- Play slow, calming music while you study.

- Sing or chant information rhythmically.

- Review out loud what you already know.

Tactile Aids:

- Use a colored pen to highlight items in a list.

- Feel anatomy or structural models with your eyes closed.

- Write key words on stick-on notes and attach them to the tips of your fingers.

- Re-do class or lecture notes by writing them cursively with a scented, flow pen.

- Associate main ideas with hot or cold temperatures or textured surfaces.

- Walk or march as you memorize key phrases.

NOTES ABOUT MY LEARNING STYLES

DECEMBER CHECKLIST

1. Register for January college courses.
2.
3. Study for December **SAT**, **ACT**, and **ACH** test dates.
4.
5. Discuss your college budget with your parents.
6.
7. Check with your counseling office for new scholarships.
8.
9. Mail your admission applications.
10.
11. Carefully review any college responses you receive.
12.
13.
14.
15. Request Financial Aid Forms from your college choices.

16	17 Decide if you wish to retake any college tests to improve scores.	18
19 Look for new award competitions to enter.	20	21 Send Certificates of Mailing for **SAT** and **ACH** January test dates.
22	23 Mail your transcripts to the colleges of your choice.	24
25 Happy Holidays!	26	27
28	29 Fill out Financial Aid Forms with your parents.	30 / 31

FINANCIAL AID HINTS

Scholarships are given for financial need, for academic achievement, and by specific ethnic groups, clubs, and fraternal or professional organizations. Ask your school counselor or counseling office to help you review those scholarships which might be appropriate for you.

There are about nineteen computer resource services to help you look for scholarships. Some are free, while others may cost you. Lists that you will receive from the services are prepared for you personally from the information you supply.

You may select lists of scholarships based on financial need alone or based upon other criteria, such as major choices, geographic location, scholarship amounts, or other specific categories. Also, you may ask your counseling office or local school board for the National Advisory Contests and Activities List which details many scholarship awards.

Most colleges and universities offer a package of scholarships, grants, and loans from which you may choose. Again, you want the greatest amount of money at the best repayment terms or with no repayment at all. If a particular school wants you, they will find the money for you. Your chances for scholarships may be better with small, rich private schools rather than large, grant-poor public institutions. Remember to explore all of your options.

Some financial aid offers may favorably surprise you!

Finding Scholarships And Financial Aid:

- Check your high school counseling office and public library for current lists.

- Request financial aid information from colleges when you ask them for admission applications.

- Survey computer resource services for prices and types of financial aid lists they offer.

- Contact local chapters of national civic, professional, and fraternal organizations.

- Get a good score on the **PSAT**, which may qualify you for National Merit Scholarships and other awards.

- Inquire about state government sponsored programs.

- Call on religious and ethnic associations and groups for help.

How to qualify for academic scholarships depends upon each type of sponsored program. Many scholarship programs require an evaluation of your Preliminary Scholastic Aptitude Test Score. You may only take the **PSAT** your junior year, so be careful to note the test date on your planning calendar. The following questions will help you keep on schedule for different types of scholarship application.

AID WORK SHEET

Have I entered National Merit competitions?

Prizes and Awards	Deadline	Date Mailed

Have I applied for state scholarships?

Prizes and Awards	Deadline	Date Mailed

Have I applied for professional scholarships?

    Names   Deadline   Date Mailed

_____

_____

Have I applied for scholarships from fraternal clubs?

    Names   Deadline   Date Mailed

_____

_____

Are there any available ethnic or religious scholarships?

    Names   Deadline   Date Mailed

_____

_____

Have I applied at "my colleges" for specific scholarships?

    Names   Deadline   Date Mailed

_____

_____

_____

_____

JANUARY CHECKLIST

1 Happy New Year!

2

3 Plan for summer jobs.

4

5

6 Request transcript updates from your high school.

7

8 Send all Financial Aid Forms by Certificates of Mailing.

9

10 Send Certificate of Mailing for **ACT** February test date.

11

12

13

14 Study for **SAT** and **ACH** tests in January.

15

16 Request any additional letters of recommendation.	**17**	**18** Request final transcripts if you are a mid-term graduate.
19	**20** Check with civic organizations for scholarship awards.	**21**
22 Check with religious and ethnic associations for scholarships.	**23**	**24** Study: Note-Taking Tips.
25	**26**	**27** Plan your senior class trip.
28	**29** Review: Note-Taking Tips.	**30** / **31**

NOTE-TAKING TIPS

For Lectures:

- Divide your paper vertically with a three-inch left margin.

- Use the three-inch space for jotting down main ideas in a few words.

- Use the larger right side space for detailing supporting information.

- Write your notes in phrases using key words, not in complete sentences.

- Draw pictures or diagrams where appropriate.

- Draw charts from final notes to help you analyze and organize ideas.

- Develop a summary which evaluates the content of the lectures.

- Draw a branching tree to evaluate complicated relationships.

For Written Material:

- Learn both Roman numeral outlining 1, 1A, 1B, 1C, etc.) and decimal outlining (1, 1.1, 1.2, 1.21, 2, 2.1, etc.) to help you organize.

- Photocopy pages and highlight topic or subject headings and key phrases.

- Use 3" x 5" index cards to write down main topics and supporting information.

- Record notes for an analysis by defining problems, causes, and solutions with proposed results.

- Write a few short paragraphs which summarize how you feel about what you have read.

- Make a list of items that need further research or clarification.

- Sketch mind maps which outline key words and phrases.

FEBRUARY CHECKLIST

1 Schedule college Advanced Placement Tests.	**2**	**3** Update your resume.
4	**5**	**6** Study for **ACT** in February.
7	**8**	**9**
10 Fill out scholarship applications.	**11** Check with your counseling office for new scholarship offerings.	**12**
13	**14**	**15** Evaluate housing choices for colleges and universities.

16	17 Plan for summer jobs.	18
19 Apply for college and university housing.	20	21 Study: Reducing Stress.
22 Enter scholarship award competitions.	23	24 Send Certificate of Mailing for **SAT** March test date.
25	26 Check that Financial Aid Form filings are complete.	27
28	29 Review: Reducing Stress.	

REDUCING STRESS

Mental Techniques:

- Clear your mind of all thoughts and breathe deeply.

- Listen to peaceful music that will cause you to relax.

- Sit or lie down comfortably; tense, then relax your muscles.

- Visualize yourself doing the things you like most.

- Envision positive, workable solutions to your problems.

- Picture yourself happy and successful.

- Remind yourself of your accomplishments.

- Learn meditation techniques or yoga.

Physical Techniques:

- Participate in your favorite sports or exercise regularly.

- Take a walk in your favorite outdoor setting.

- Talk openly to good friends and loved ones.

- Ask for a massage, take a hot bath, or get a hug.

- Attend a play, movie, or stimulating cultural event.

- Eat a diet rich in natural vitamins, free of drugs and alcohol.

MARCH CHECKLIST

1 Final deadline for Financial Aid Forms to be mailed.

2

3

4

5 Schedule follow-up college campus visits.

6

7

8

9 Send Certificate of Mailing for **ACT** April test date.

10

11

12 Start looking for summer school opportunities.

13 Enter award competitions.

14

15

16	17 Continue looking for summer jobs.	18
19	20	21 Study: Research Skills.
22 Study for March **SAT**.	23	24
25	26 Send Certificates of Mailing for **SAT** and **ACH** May test dates.	27
28	29 Review: Research Skills.	30 / 31

USING RESEARCH SKILLS

Searching For Information:

- Write an outline , organizing the information you wish to research.

- Research for facts by thinking about which encyclopedias, books, or magazines may have information.

- Use bibliographies in encyclopedias and your text books for reference.

- Evaluate an author's or a publication's credibility and biases on your specific topic.

Finding Information:

- Learn to use your library's card catalog and The Reader's Guide.

- Use library computers to access books, indices, and periodicals.

- Ask the reference desk for additional sources of information.

- Find out which libraries near you have special reference and rare book sections.

- Write or call trade and government information services for supplements.

Documenting Information:

- Use 3" x 5" index cards that you may re-arrange later to complete outlines.

- Write down the author's name and the source's title, place, and date of publication.

- Use acceptable bibliography and footnote styles.

- Write a comprehensive bibliography listing for each source before you begin reading them.

- Footnote each statement of fact or opinion and reference a page number for each.

- Store information you wish to retain on a computer database.

- Remember to move footnotes with the appropriate data as you re-page documents.

APRIL CHECKLIST

1 Study for April **ACT**.	**2**	**3** Review community college opportunities and mail completed applications.
4	**5** Compare financial aid offers from your college choices.	**6**
7	**8**	**9** Check with your counseling office for new scholarships.
10	**11** Continue looking for summer jobs and opportunity programs.	**12**
13	**14**	**15** Review acceptance notices from colleges and universities.

16 Study: Problem Solving.	17	18 Mail your college or university housing application and deposits.
19	20	21 Write your letter of acceptance to the college of your choice and mail it.
22 Send Certificates of Mailing for May Advanced Placement Tests.	23	24
25 Send Certificates of Mailing for **SAT** and **ACH** June test dates.	26	27 Review: Problem Solving.
28	29 Write letters of refusal to colleges you did not select.	30

PROBLEM SOLVING

Identifying The Problem:

- State your problem in one general sentence.

- Analyze your problem using "who, what, when, where, why, and how."

- Divide your problem into component or sub-problems and choose the easiest aspects to work on first.

Gaining Perspective:

- Combine or substitute elements of the problem to hint at solutions.

- Eliminate elements or add new elements to view the problem differently.

- Sleep on a problem and approach it with a fresh point of view the next day.

- Brainstorm all creative solutions and don't throw out any too soon.

- Define your criteria by determining the best solution from all of your choices.

- List the pros and cons of all possibilities.

- Use the criteria and your list to pick the most viable solution.

- Select two or three alternative solutions.

Implementing A Solution:

- Define who, what, when, where, why, why, and how a solution will be implemented.

- Prioritize tasks. What is the first step? Is there anything you need to do before you start that? And before that?

- Write an action plan with a time line stating in order, what you are going to do, with whom, and when, where, why, and how you are going to do it.

- Review the plan as it is implemented and revise it when necessary.

MAY CHECKLIST

1 Write your letter of acceptance. Congratulations!

2

3 Study for May **SAT** and **ACH**.

4

5 Write thank you notes to teachers and others who recommended you.

6

7 Mail graduation invitations.

8

9 Take placement exams for community colleges.

10

11 Send Certificate of Mailing for **ACT** June test date.

12

13

14

15 Decide on a summer job.

16	17 Check all Advanced Placement Test dates.	18
19	20 Study for finals.	21
22 Request a final transcript for the college or university you will attend.	23	24 Study: Reading Skills.
25	26 Study for finals.	27
28	29 Review: Reading Skills.	30 / 31

READING SKILLS

Getting An Overview:

- Decide your purpose for reading a particular piece of material, whether you are reading for pleasure, information, or to learn something.

- Look over the material, including the covers, table of contents, chapter headings, and pictures.

- Outline what you have observed and decide how much time you wish to spend on the material.

As You Read:

- Use your hand or fingers to help you focus your eye movements and increase your speed.

- Read at a brisk pace and concentrate.

- Go back and review the material for main points and important details.

- Write down short notes with supporting details to aid your memory if your purpose is learning.

- Outline as you go by writing main ideas on the left side of a page. Indent to the right for supporting arguments and facts.

Evaluating Material:

- Ask yourself if you accomplished your original purpose in reading the material.

- Review your notes to see if they are complete.

- Write questions which were not answered that you wish to research.

- Analyze the author's motives and bias in presenting the topic.

- Highlight areas of agreement or disagreement.

JUNE CHECKLIST

1 Study for **SAT**, **ACH**, and **ACT** in June.

2

3

4

5

6

7

8 Send any follow-up information requested by the college you will attend.

9

10

11

12

13

14

15 Check that your final transcript was sent; get a copy for your files.

16	17	18
19	20 Send thank you notes for graduation gifts.	21
22	23	24
25	26 Thank your parents for their support!	27
28	29	30

SUMMARY

College Countdown is intended as a guide to assist parents and students through the maze of paperwork and scheduling challenges involved in preparing for college.

Although unique in its conceptual approach, *College Countdown* has been written to supplement other college entry books of substantial quality. A partial list of those books easily available though high school and public libraries or through bookstores appears in the adjacent bibliography.

Every effort has been made to make *College Countdown* complete, accurate, and current up to the date of publication. No representations, either express or implied, are made or given regarding the consequences of the use of any information contained in this book. The publisher, author, editors, designers, distributors, and all other persons or entities associated with the creation, preparation, publication, sale, or distribution of *College Countdown* shall in no event have any liability to the reader for any direct, indirect, incidental, special, or consequential damages arising out of the use of the information, the lack of information, or any inferences in this book.

Comments and suggestions on the form and content of *College Countdown* should be addressed to the author at the address which appears on the opening legend of this book.

BIBLIOGRAPHY

Choosing A College:

- American College Testing Staff.
  College Planning Search Book.
  27th ed., American College Testing, 1991.
- Beckham, Barry.
  College Selection Workbook.
  Beckham House, 1990.
- Blaker, Charles W.
  The College Matchmaker.
  Rekalf Press, 1980.
- Cahn, Victor.
  A Thinking Student's Guide to College.
  Chris Mass, 1988.
- College Board Staff.
  Index of Majors 1991.
  College Board, 1990.
- College Division Staff.
  Barron's Indices to College Majors,
  17th ed., Barron's, 1990.
- College Division Staff.
  Barron's Profiles of American Colleges,
  17th ed., Barron's, 1990.
- Data Notes Publishing Staff.
  Colleges That Offer Credit For Life Experience. Data, 1983.
- Eaton, Judith.
  Colleges of Choice.
  ACE, 1987.

- Featherstone, Bonnie D. and Reilly, Jill M.
  College Comes Sooner Than You Think,
  Ohio Psychology Press, 1990.
- Fiske, Edward B. and Michalak, Moseph M.
  The Best Buys In College Education.
  Random House, 1985.
- Leans, Frank.
  Getting Into College.
  FS & G., 1990.
- Marius, Richard, and Weiner, Harvey S.
  The McGraw-Hill College Handbook.
  2nd ed., McGraw-Hill, 1988.
- Miller, Gordon P.
  Choosing A College.
  College Board., 1990.
- Nemko, Martin.
  How To Get An Ivy League Education At A State University.
  Avon, 1988.
- Peterson Press.
  Peterson's Guide To Four-Year Colleges.
  21st ed., Peterson's Guides, 1990.
- Roes, Nicholas A.
  America's Lowest Cost Colleges.
  6th ed., NAR Productions, 1989.
- Sowell, Thomas.
  Choosing A College.
  Harper-Collins, 1989.

- Steinbrecher, Phyllis and Ryan, Elizabeth.
Getting Into The College Of Your Choice.
Putnam, 1987.
- Straughn II, Charles T. and Barbara Sue.
Lovejoy's College Guide.
19th ed., Monarch Press, 1989.

Financial Aid:

- Blum, Laurie.
Free Money For Colleges.
Facts On File.
- Bowman, Linda.
How To Get To College For Free.
Probus, 1991.
- Brownstone, David M. and Hawes, Gene R.
The College Money Book.
Macmillan, 1984.
- Broyles, Susan G.
College Costs: Basic Student Charges At Two-Year and Four-Year Institutions.
USGPO, 1990.
- Chronicle Guides.
Chronicle Student Aid Annual.
Chronicle Guides, 1990.
- Dennis, Marguerite.
Barron's Complete College Financing Guide.
Barron's, 1989.

- Dilts, Susan W.
Peterson's College Money Handbook.
Peterson's, 1990.
- Edelstein, Scott and Consumer Reports Book Editors.
Putting Your Kids Through College.
Consumer Reports, 1989.
- Fenske, Robert H. et al, eds.
Handbook Of Student Financial Aid.
Bks. Demain UMI.
- Fiske, Edward B. and Michalak, Joseph M.
The Best Buys In College Education.
Random House, 1985.
- Gladhart, Peter M.
Student Financial Survival Guide.
Kendall-Hunt, 1989.
- Hauptman, Arthur.
New Ways Of Paying For College.
ACE, 1991.
- Kerfetz, Gerald.
How To Pay For Your Children's College.
College Board, 1988.
- Unknown.
Lovejoy's Guide To Financial Aid.
3rd ed., ARCO, 1989.
- Macmillan Editors.
The College Blue Book: Scholarships, Fellowships, Grants and Loans.
Macmillan , 1979.

- Margohn, F. B.
  College Financial Aid Annual 1989.
  ARCO, 1988.
- Stewart, Jayme.
  How To Get Into The College Of Your Choice And How To Finance It.
  Morrow, 1991.

Scholastic Aptitude Tests:

- Unknown.
  Barron's How To Prepare For The Scholastic Aptitude Test - SAT.
  15th ed., Barron's, 1989.
- Carris, Joan D., et al.
  SAT Success: Peterson's Study Guide To English And Math Skills For College Entrance Examinations.
  Peterson's, 1987, revised.
- College Board Staff.
  The College Board Guide To Preparing For The PSAT And NMSQ.
  College Board, 1988.

- College Board Staff.
Ten SAT's.
College Board, 1988.
- Depula, Edward.
Preparation For The SAT: Scholastic AptitudeTest.
ARCO, 1987.
- Gruber, Gary.
Gruber's Complete Preparation For The SAT.
4th ed., Harper-Collins, 1990.
- Lebow, Allen, et. al.
Barron's Computer Study Program For The SAT.
2nd ed., Apple and IBM versions, Barron's, 1989.
- Unknown.
Lovejoy's Preparation For The SAT.
S and S Trade, 1985.
- Saunders, Bridgette.
Mathematics Workbook For The SAT.
ARCO, 1990.
- Saunders, Bridgette, et., al.
Scholastic Aptitude Test.
5th ed., ARCO, 1984.
- Unknown.
Taking The SAT: A Guide To Taking The Scholastic Aptitude Test and The Test Of Standard Written English.
College Board, 1990.

"*College Countdown* is in a class by itself! It's the clearest, simplest, most comprehensive guide for high school students. Helen Heron gave me the tools for entry into a Top Ten college."

Chris Fagan,
Microsoft

"...A month-by-month survival manual for families tackling the chore of college application, presenting the application and scholarship process in a simple, straight forward manner."

Pomona College Alumni Magazine, 1990

"*College Countdown* is truly excellent. A wealth of information, tips, in an easy-to-follow, calendar format. It's great! The study skills are what every high school student needs to know to succeed."

Roy L. Jones,
Fellow, Creative Problem Solving Institute

"All high school students should be given *College Countdown* when they enter the 9th grade. It's about time someone cared enough to think through college preparation from a student's point of view."

Dorris Lee,
Author, *The Reader's Edge*

NOTES TO REMEMBER

NOTES TO REMEMBER

NOTES TO REMEMBER

NOTES TO REMEMBER

NOTES TO REMEMBER

FUNDRAISING

College Countdown is also available in workbook form for charity and fundraising events and organizations. Workbooks are 8 1/2" x 11" and are spiral bound for convenience and to reduce the price per unit.

Order forms and public relations information on how to set up a successful fundraiser may be requested from the distributor.

In addition, high school students may request information on how to sell *College Countdown* workbooks to supplement their financial resources for attending colleges and universities.

Please address all inquiries to the distributor at the address which appears below:

- *College Countdown*
  c/o **Momentum Associates, Ltd.**
  Post Office Box 12266
  Glendale, CA 91224-0966

6/30/94